HOW CAN WE SAVE OUR WORLD?

sustainable
CITIES

Angela Royston

FRANKLIN WATTS
LONDON · SYDNEY

First published in 2009 by Franklin Watts

Copyright © 2009 Arcturus Publishing Limited

Franklin Watts
338 Euston Road
London NW1 3BH

Franklin Watts Australia
Level 17/207 Kent Street
Sydney, NSW 2000

Produced by Arcturus Publishing Limited
26/27 Bickels Yard
151–153 Bermondsey Street
London SE1 3HA

The right of Angela Royston to be identified as the author of this work has been asserted by her in accordance with the Copyright, Designs and Patents Act 1988.

All rights reserved

Series concept: Alex Woolf
Editor and picture researcher: Cath Senker
Designer: Phipps Design
Consultant: Howard Sharman, Univerity College London

A CIP catalogue record for this book is available from the British Library.

Dewey Decimal Classification Number: 307.76

ISBN 978 0 7496 8211 8

Printed in China

Franklin Watts is a division of Hachette Children's Books, an Hachette UK company.
www.hachette.co.uk

Picture Credits
Chris Fairclough Worldwide: 28 (Edward Parker), 31 (Edward Parker), 33 (John Birdsall), 41 (Chris Fairclough).
Corbis: 6 (Jed Leicester/Reuters), 8 (Diego Lezama Orezzoli), 14 (Ciro Fusco/epa), 17 (Smiley N. Pool/Dallas Morning News), 19 (Michael Freeman), 26 (Eric Sierins), 32 (Michael S. Yamashita).
EASI-Images (all Rob Bowden except where indicated) 11 (Simon Scoones), 12, 13, 15, 18, 21 (Miguel Hunt), 25 (Adrian Cooper), 27, 29, 34 (Adrian Cooper), 36, 37 (Neal Cavalier-Smith), 38, 39, 40.
Jerry Harrall: 23.
Rex Features: cover.
Robert Royston: 43.
Science Photo Library (Gary Hincks): 16.
Shutterstock: 7 (Shawn Kashou), 9 (nikolpetr), 30 (Otmar Smit).

The artwork on pages 10, 16 and 22 is by Phipps Design.

Cover picture
This house in New Mexico, USA is energy self-sufficient, with a wind turbine and solar water heater.

Credits
Every attempt has been made to clear copyright. Should there be any inadvertent omission please apply to the publisher for rectification.

CONTENTS

INTRODUCTION
The Pull of the City — 6

CHAPTER 1
Cities in History — 8

CHAPTER 2
Why Cities are Unsustainable — 12

CHAPTER 3
Sustainable Building — 18

CHAPTER 4
Eco-Communities — 26

CHAPTER 5
Making Existing Cities Greener — 30

CHAPTER 6
Getting Around the City — 36

CHAPTER 7
Better for Everyone — 42

Glossary — 44

Further Information — 45

Index — 46

INTRODUCTION

The Pull of the City

Cities all over the world are growing ever bigger: some are so big they join together, creating vast megacities. Cities cover the natural landscape with bricks, concrete and tar. They suck in huge amounts of resources and spew out large amounts of rubbish. So why do people want to live in cities?

A better life

People come to cities looking for excitement and opportunity. Cities have more colleges, shops, theatres, cinemas, restaurants, clubs and music venues than other places. Nevertheless, most people migrate to cities to find work. Cities provide thousands of different jobs, for example in shops, offices and factories. Capital cities contain government offices, too. The best-paid and most powerful jobs are usually city-based and draw in well-qualified people from all over the world. Poor people also flock to cities looking for any work they can find.

Many cities have a diverse population. They include people and cultures from many countries. This is the Notting Hill Carnival in London, UK, a Caribbean festival attended by hundreds of thousands of people.

FACE THE **FACTS**

Tokyo-Yokohama in Japan is the world's largest city by population. More than 34 million people live there. Tokyo-Yokohama is really two cities that have joined to form one. The world's largest city by area is New York. Together with the surrounding towns it has engulfed, the city covers more than 11,000 square kilometres.

City needs

More people live in cities than ever before. Just over half the world's population now lives in urban areas, and about half of urban dwellers live in cities of more than 500,000 people. Each large city consumes hundreds of thousands of tonnes of food, millions of litres of water and gigawatts of electricity every day. These are usually brought in from outside. Consumer goods, petrol and some foods may even come from the other side of the world.

Are cities sustainable?

Many people are now realizing that cities damage the environment – not just the countryside over which they sprawl, but the world environment, too. Resources, such as water, food, fuel and raw materials, are not limitless. City life is unsustainable when the city uses resources faster than they can be replaced. Architects and planners are beginning to think again about how cities operate and how they can be made more sustainable.

Skyscrapers consume vast amounts of building materials and they are getting taller. Burj Dubai (right), completed in 2009, is about twice the height of the previously tallest buildings, the Petronas Towers in Kuala Lumpur, Malaysia.

CHAPTER 1

Cities in History

Cities became possible only after agriculture was invented about 10,000 years ago in Mesopotamia, in what is now Iraq. By planting crops and herding animals, farmers produced more food than they needed.

Farmers sold their surplus, allowing other people to give up farming and become craftsmen and traders. People lived together in villages and began to rely on each other for the things they needed. Farming and trade spread to other regions, and some villages grew into cities.

Early cities

By 4000 BC the populations of the largest cities, such as Ur and Sumer, had grown to about 25,000. The most powerful and wealthy people built temples, palaces and magnificent houses in the centre of the city. Poorer people lived around the edge, while outside the city walls were the farmers who grew and sold food to the urban population. Early cities also developed in Egypt, China and India, and later in Greece, Rome and Central America.

Mohenjo-Daro was built in about 2500 BC in the Indus Valley in what is now Pakistan. It was built on a grid pattern and is the first example of city planning.

Many were built on the banks of rivers, which provided them with water, drainage and an easy way to move goods in and out by ship.

Medieval cities

Most medieval cities were surrounded by a strong wall. The wall protected the city from attack but it also limited its size. The wealthiest cities made their money from trade and so were usually built on rivers or on the coast. Goods, made by people in small workshops, were sold locally and sometimes to distant countries. As trade thrived and the population increased, cities spread beyond their walls. The biggest cities, such as Venice in Italy, London in England and Antwerp in the Netherlands, had several hundred thousand inhabitants.

PERSPECTIVE

Marco Polo (c.1254–1324)

Marco Polo was a great Venetian traveller and one of the first Europeans to visit China. Here he describes the city of Hangzhou:

'The city is beyond dispute the finest and the noblest in the world.... And there are in it twelve thousand bridges of stone, for the most part so lofty that a great fleet could pass beneath them.... Inside the city there is a Lake ... and all round it are erected beautiful palaces and mansions, of the richest and most exquisite structure that you can imagine, belonging to the nobles of the city.'

As cities became centres of power and wealth, they needed to defend themselves from attack. People in the castle in Carcassonne, France, defended the city.

SUSTAINABLE CITIES

The staggering rise of cities

The population of cities increased dramatically in the nineteenth century. The expansion began in Britain with the Industrial Revolution, which followed James Watt's invention of the steam engine in 1765. Steam engines were used in mines and factories, and to pull trains. This invention was just the first of many new machines that transformed society and cities.

Factories using the new machines produced huge numbers of cheap goods and employed many people. Industrialization soon spread to other European countries and to North America. Towns grew up close to coalmines and quickly grew larger. People moved from the countryside to find work in the factories. They lived in overcrowded slums, in streets that were blackened by smoke from the factory chimneys.

FACE THE FACTS

This chart shows the growth of the urban population in each continent since 1950, and the predicted percentage of the population that will live in cities in 2030.

Area	Per cent of the population living in urban areas
World	1950: ~30, 2007: ~50, 2030: ~60
Africa	1950: ~15, 2007: ~38, 2030: ~50
Asia	1950: ~17, 2007: ~41, 2030: ~54
Europe	1950: ~52, 2007: ~72, 2030: ~78
Latin America/Caribbean	1950: ~42, 2007: ~76, 2030: ~84
North America	1950: ~64, 2007: ~81, 2030: ~87
Oceania	1950: ~62, 2007: ~71, 2030: ~74

Key: Per cent urban 1950 ■ Per cent urban 2007 ■ Per cent urban 2030 (predicted)

Source: United Nations, World Urbanization Prospects: The 2005 Revision (2006) and Carl Haub, 2007 World Population Data Sheet.

Gradually, city environments grew better. Factory owners were forced to improve working hours and conditions. An understanding of how germs cause disease led to better sewerage systems and safer hospitals. The invention of electricity brought electric lights and machinery. The first oil well, drilled in 1859, led to the invention of the petrol engine. The earliest cars took to the road in the 1890s, and the first powered aircraft flew in 1904.

Cities in the twentieth century

Oil provided fuel for transport by road, rail, sea and air. Communications between and within cities increased and became faster. This meant that people could live further from the city centre and commute to work. New materials and building methods transformed city buildings. Skyscraper office blocks now dominate most city centres; they would not have been possible without Elisha Otis's safety lift and the invention of air conditioning. Cities expanded fast. By 2000 there were 388 cities with more than a million inhabitants, but the United Nations predicts that by 2015 there will be 21 megacities with populations of 10 million or more.

A view towards the ocean from Rochina favela (shanty town) in Rio de Janeiro. Much of the urban population growth in poorer countries is in shanty towns.

FACE THE FACTS

The fastest-growing cities are in developing countries. In those places, people migrate to cities hoping to find work, better schools and hospitals, and a higher standard of living. In reality they usually end up in shanty towns on the edge of cities. Shanty towns often have no clean water, sewerage systems or electricity. People build their own homes out of materials such as corrugated iron and cardboard.

CHAPTER 2

Why Cities are Unsustainable

People need shelter, food and consumer goods, water and power, but most city-dwellers have little idea where these supplies come from, or what happens to their rubbish and sewage.

As the population of cities grows, new homes have to be built, using concrete, iron, glass, wood and other raw materials. Clean water pours from the taps, and dirty water disappears into the drains. Electricity – usually generated in distant power stations – is laid on and available at the flick of a switch. It is easy to buy food, clothes and other goods from city shops. The labels may reveal that the goods have come from China, Brazil, Kenya or Spain, for example, but they do not tell you how much fuel and resources were used to transport them.

People come from miles around to shop at huge shopping centres, such as this fashionable shopping area in Tokyo, Japan. Most people arrive by car, using fuel and causing pollution. Large areas of land may be concreted over to provide parking space for their cars.

Why Cities are Unsustainable

PERSPECTIVE

Need or greed?

Indian philosopher and political leader Mahatma Gandhi said that 'Earth provides enough to satisfy every man's need, but not every man's greed.' World population has tripled since Gandhi's death in 1948, making it ever more urgent that we find ways of providing a good standard of living without draining the earth's resources. Gandhi also said 'Be the change you want to see in the world.'

Ecological footprint

Researchers have devised a way of measuring the impact of a city on the environment. It is called its ecological footprint. This is the area of land needed to supply the city and dispose of the rubbish. The researchers calculate that the earth has enough resources to sustain an area equivalent to 1.7 hectares per person. The current level of consumption, however, is 2.3 hectares. This means that people are already consuming resources faster than our planet can replace them.

Cities in rich countries have the largest ecological footprints. For example, it has been calculated that London relies on an area of land that is 120 times bigger than London itself. This amounts to about 20 million hectares, or about 3 hectares per person. Residents in New York and Boston, in the United States, require even more – 8.4 hectares of land per person – to maintain their current way of life. This is at least ten times greater than a similar-sized city in India.

A new high-rise building under construction in Tokyo, Japan. The huge amounts of raw materials needed to complete the building will be brought in by lorry, often from distant factories.

SUSTAINABLE CITIES

Disposing of waste

A city produces thousands of tonnes of rubbish every day. Dustbins and litterbins are emptied regularly. Most of the rubbish is dumped in landfill sites – huge holes dug in the ground on the edge or outside of the city. Much of the rubbish is made up of plastic and other materials that do not rot, but remain in the ground for hundreds of years. Apart from polluting the land, many countries are rapidly running out of space for landfill. Huge incinerators are an alternative to landfill, but burning rubbish can produce poisonous gases that pollute the air.

Bags of rubbish were piled high in the streets of Naples in Italy after rubbish collectors refused to collect it during a dispute in 2008. Problems like this make people aware of the amount of rubbish cities produce.

Sewage

Rubbish isn't the only waste that people produce. Sewage is carried away in underground pipes, except in most shanty towns, where sewage may run through open ditches. A hygienic sewerage system is not the end of the story, however. If the sewage is allowed to flow into rivers or the sea, it causes pollution. Sewage farms filter out the waste, clean up the water and may even turn the remains into fertilizer.

Polluting the air and water

Cities produce tonnes of waste gases that pollute the air. The gases come mainly from traffic, factories and power stations. Some of the pollution is invisible, although it may show up as photochemical smog when the sun shines. Other pollution is clearly visible. Many cities are constantly shrouded in haze or, worse still, thick smog. Although pollution may hang over a city, it is also blown by the wind, sometimes hundreds of kilometres. Lakes and forests in Scandinavia are dying because of rain that has been polluted by smoke and exhaust gases produced by distant cities.

Air pollution is so bad in Tokyo, Japan, that this cycle attendant is wearing a mask to filter out the harmful gases.

PERSPECTIVE

Face to face with sewage

On the Around the World website, Joe Atkins, a sewage worker in New York, USA, recalls when he first started work: 'The early days on the job were the hard ones. I remember coming home from work, knocked out from inhaling methane, and falling asleep. I was unprepared for the experience of dealing with raw sewage and rats.'

Roger Alva had learnt to keep his mouth tightly shut in the sewers, but occasionally a splash of filthy water went astray. Then he had to rinse his mouth with a special type of alcohol.

Global warming

There is an even more urgent reason why cities need to become sustainable. The temperature at the surface of the earth is rising. This is called global warming and, although the average rise since 1750 is, at present, less than 1° C, it is already dramatically altering weather patterns. Climates are becoming unpredictable and hurricanes, droughts and floods are becoming more severe. What is causing global warming?

Greenhouse gases

Greenhouse gases are gases in the air, such as carbon dioxide and methane, that trap the sun's heat, making the earth warmer. We need some greenhouse gases to keep the earth at the right temperature to support the wide variety of life that exists now. The problem is that man-made greenhouse gases are increasing, trapping more of the sun's heat. The main greenhouse gas is carbon dioxide, which is produced when people burn coal, oil and natural gas. These fuels are called fossil fuels because they formed millions of years ago from the remains of plants and tiny sea animals. As they formed, they locked up carbon. When the fuel is burned, the carbon is released.

About half of the sun's heat is absorbed by the earth's surface. This heat then radiates back into the atmosphere, but greenhouse gases trap and reflect some of it, making the surface of the earth warmer.

The greenhouse effect

1) Heat from the sun's rays enters the earth's atmosphere.

2) The surface of the earth radiates back the heat.

3) Most of the radiated heat goes back into space.

4) Some of the heat is absorbed by carbon dioxide in the atmosphere and remains there. This makes the earth hotter.

How cities contribute to global warming

Cities burn fossil fuels in many different ways. Road transport relies on petrol and diesel, which are both made from oil. The energy to heat and cool buildings is usually generated by burning fossil fuels. Most of the food sold in city shops has been sprayed with pesticides and fertilizers made from oil.

The way ahead

There are ways to make cities more sustainable. Architects need to rethink the way they construct new buildings, in particular which materials they use and where the materials come from. Buildings should be designed so that they use less energy for heating and lighting. Instead of travelling long distances across the city to work, communities can be planned so that more people can work nearer home.

In 2005 the US city of New Orleans was flooded following Hurricane Katrina. The flood occurred because the city's flood defences had been poorly maintained. As floods become more common, cities will have to spend an increasing amount of money on flood defences.

FACE THE FACTS

The more the earth warms, the greater the consequences. Scientists predict that an increase of just 2° C above 1750 levels would, among other things, threaten a quarter of all species with extinction, put 90 to 200 million more people at risk of catching malaria, and make between 226 million and 2 billion more people short of water.

CHAPTER 3

Sustainable Building

As well as shelter from wind and rain, a building has to provide heating in cold weather and cooling in hot weather. It needs electricity to power computers, lighting and other devices, and it requires clean water and a system for dealing with rubbish and sewage.

Some homes have been built that do all this without producing greenhouse gases or damaging the environment. These 'eco-homes' provide blueprints for the future. Eco-homes are built with materials that are found locally and are renewable. Waste and recycled materials satisfy both of these conditions. For example, Earthships are eco-homes designed and built by architect Michael Reynolds in the Arizona Desert, USA. The main building blocks are used tyres filled with earth. The tyres are stacked up and covered with mud so you cannot see them. Old cans, cardboard and recycled glass and wood are also used.

The UK's first Earthship, which was opened in Fife, Scotland, in 2004 as a demonstration centre. Built with the assistance of Michael Reynolds, it shows how sustainable building techniques can be adopted locally.

Some Earthships look extraordinary, but sustainable materials can also be used to build more normal-looking homes. They are built with natural materials that are found locally, such as stone and mud. They use wood that comes from managed forests, in which fast-growing trees provide timber, and new trees are grown to replace them.

Glorious mud

Mud is a good building material because it is easily available and insulates against heat and cold. It is used in traditional building methods in many parts of the world. Adobe consists of mud mixed with straw and left in the sun to harden. Mud can also be mixed with cement to make a kind of lightweight concrete. Alternatively, it can be pressed into shape to make thick walls of rammed (compressed) earth.

PERSPECTIVE

Ideal home

Eco-architects claim that eco-homes take advantage of all climates. If it rains, the water is collected. If it is windy, the wind turbine generates electricity. If it is sunny, more electricity is generated. 'Imagine a home,' Michael Reynolds told *The Independent* newspaper, 'that heats itself, that provides its own water, and grows its own food. Imagine that it needs no expensive technology, it recycles its own waste, and it has its own power source. And now imagine that it can be built anywhere, by anyone, out of the things that society throws away.'

This traditional building, called a *pueblo*, in Taos, New Mexico, is made of adobe and blends in with its surroundings. The building has a wooden frame made of strong beams that extend beyond the walls. The mud walls are damaged by the weather and have to be replaced from time to time. The wooden frame, however, remains.

Generating electricity

Eco-homes produce electricity using wind and sunlight – neither of which will run out. The force of the wind turns the blades of a wind turbine to generate electricity. Wind turbines work best in places that have a steady wind most of the time, such as on the coast or lakeside, on hilltops or plains. They work less well in cities, which are usually more sheltered.

Photovoltaic (PV) cells contain silicon crystals that generate electricity from sunlight. The cells are about the same size as roof tiles and usually replace tiles on the side of the roof that catches the most sunlight. PV cells perform best in bright, sunny places, but they also work in cloudy, dull conditions. They do not, of course, work at night. Between them, PV cells and a wind turbine can provide enough electricity to power the lights, computers and other machines in a home. Once installed, they produce no greenhouse gases.

At present PV cells are costly to buy. They also have to be kept clean so that sunlight can easily penetrate them. A recent development is to use PV cells in window frames. They are much cheaper and more efficient (see page 31). PV cells work best in hot, sunny countries, but they can also work well in cooler, cloudier countries.

SUSTAINABLE TECHNOLOGIES

Hydrogen fuel cells

In the future, the most efficient way of generating electricity is likely to be a hydrogen fuel cell. The cell combines hydrogen and oxygen to produce water, electricity and heat. A fuel cell can work well with PV cells. During the day, excess electricity from the PV cells is used to produce hydrogen from water. At night the fuel cell uses the hydrogen to generate electricity.

Solar heating

An eco-home is built to take advantage of the sun's heat. Solar water heaters on the roof heat the water. The building has large windows that face the sun to take in heat on cool days. This is called passive solar heating. With good design and insulation (see page 22), very little extra heat is needed in winter, but a wood-burning stove can be used if necessary. Trees or awnings shelter the same windows in summer, when the aim is to keep the inside cool.

Heat pumps

Heat pumps make use of a difference in temperature between two places, either inside and outside a building, or the temperature at ground level compared with several metres underground. A heat pump transfers heat from one place – usually the warmer place – to the cooler place. The system works best when the difference in temperature is not too large.

(opposite) Solar cells can be used on existing buildings as well as on new buildings. The dark panels on the walls of this block of flats in Berlin in Germany are PV cells that generate electricity for the flats.

Insulating a house

- Attic
- Storage space
- Side wall
- Triple-glazed windows
- Ceiling
- Double-glazed windows
- Foundations
- Basement

The best way to insulate a house is to cocoon it by laying insulating material under the ground floor, on all of the outside walls and in the attic. Double or triple glazing insulates the windows. In this diagram, the layers of insulation are shown in pink.

Insulation

Insulation keeps a building warm in winter and cool in summer. Some eco-homes use earth and plants to insulate the building from the outside. This mimics the burrows of animals, such as rabbits and gerbils, which survive extreme heat or cold by living underground. Traditional thatch also insulates the roof. A more conventional way to insulate a building is to put insulating material between the top floor and the roof, and on the outer wall of the building. However, many insulating materials are synthetic, which means that many of them are made from oil. Homes that are completely carbon free use a natural material, such as sheep's wool.

Double glazing and draught-proofing

Windows let in light, but they also allow heat to escape. Double-glazed windows lose much less heat because they have two panes of glass with air, or better still argon gas, between them. Triple-glazed windows have three panes of glass and lose even less heat. Warm air also escapes around windows and doors unless the gaps are sealed with foam or brushes. This is called draught-proofing. Insulation, double-glazing and draught-proofing can save 30 per cent of the energy used to heat a building.

Natural ventilation

Instead of having air conditioning in summer, new homes can be designed to be cool and use natural ventilation. Many of the techniques are copied from traditional buildings in hot countries. In these places, homes are often built around a shady courtyard and have few windows on the outside walls. Windcatchers are based on a traditional idea, but have been adapted to modern buildings. A windcatcher is a double vent in the roof. Hot air from the building rises and escapes through one vent, while fresh, cool air is drawn down the other vent to replace it.

PERSPECTIVE

The Hobbit house

Jerry Harrall built an earthshelter for his family in Lincolnshire, UK. He told *The Guardian* newspaper, 'Occasionally we get called Hobbits, but we're not underground – we're in a bungalow covered in earth. I think we've created an environment of serenity and tranquillity. One side faces south with a lot of glass, so we have a high level of daylight. The rest, including the roof, is covered in earth planted with ivy, which reduces the rate of heat loss and acts as sound-proofing. Although we have no heating, the temperature remains between 18 and 21° C.'

Jerry Harrall's earthshelter is built of heavyweight material that stores heat. The outside is covered with a type of polystyrene that acts as a super insulator.

SUSTAINABLE CITIES

Reducing demand for water

In many cities, water is in short supply. As a city grows larger, its demand for water increases, but the supply may not be able to keep pace. Some cities, such as Melbourne in Australia, are also suffering from increasing drought owing to climate change. Water is wasted, too. In most countries, tap water is filtered and cleaned so that it is safe to drink. Yet most of this costly clean water is used in toilets and flushed down the drains! Cities need to use much less water.

Saving water

Eco-home owners save water in several ways. They collect rainwater in a water butt or tank, and recycle bath water, washing-machine water and other 'grey' water. In some eco-homes, this water is filtered several times so that it is safe to drink, but most people simply use grey water for flushing toilets and watering the garden. Other ways of saving water are also encouraged, such as having a shower or a smaller bath. Toilets, dishwashers and washing machines are chosen to use as little water and as little energy as possible.

SUSTAINABLE TECHNOLOGIES

Compost toilet

One of the simplest ways to deal with sewage is to have a compost toilet. There are many different designs available, but the purpose of all of them is to turn human sewage into compost that can be used to enrich the soil. Dry composting toilets do not use water and so are useful in areas that often have droughts. The technology for composting toilets is improving, so that the smell is reduced and less space is needed to compost the sewage. Compost toilets are particularly useful in places that are not connected to the sewerage system.

Closer to nature

Most sustainable housing includes a garden or shared gardens. These provide a space that usually includes trees and a pond or running water. Some have roof gardens as well as ground-level gardens. Studies have shown that people benefit from being in touch with nature. It relieves stress and keeps them in touch with the changing seasons.

Sustainable Building

Gardens are also used for growing food. Many eco-home owners are able to grow most of the vegetables they need and some of the fruit. Turning sewage into compost provides free fertilizer and allows them to produce organic food, grown without artificial chemicals.

This roof garden on top of a building in Beijing in China provides a peaceful escape from the busy streets below. Its plants may also help to soak up some of the city's pollution and improve the air quality.

CHAPTER 4

Eco-Communities

Cities in many different countries have built eco-communities. For example, Freiburg in Germany has a sustainable community of 5,000 homes. Australia's Olympic Village, originally built for the 2000 Olympic Games in Sydney, has been developed into a green suburb with many sustainable features.

Some countries plan to build whole new eco-towns, but many people think that these plans are too ambitious. In 2008, for example, Britain's plan to build up to ten new eco-towns, each housing about 30,000 people, was cut down to just two towns. China has the biggest plan of all – for Dongtan, a city for one million people, powered entirely by renewable energy. Whatever their size, eco-communities use many of the same ideas as eco-homes, but the planners have to find ways of making transport and other systems sustainable, too.

The Olympic Village in Sydney is now an eco-community. The buildings face the midday sun so they benefit from passive solar heating in winter. Awnings shade the windows in summer.

Hammarby Sjöstad is a large eco-community that is being built on a brownfield site in Stockholm in Sweden. When it is completed in 2010 it will provide flats and work spaces for about 30,000 people on land that was once used for docks and industry.

Generating extra electricity

Photovoltaic cells and rooftop wind turbines may not provide enough electricity for an entire community. A combined heat and power (CHP) station is an efficient way of generating electricity locally. In a conventional power station, much of the energy available in the fuel is lost as heat. In a CHP station, the waste heat is used to heat water that is piped into local buildings for central heating. Some CHP stations burn natural gas, which produces less carbon dioxide than burning coal or oil. In an eco-town, the CHP station may burn wood chips or organic farm waste.

Transport links

Eco-towns and communities aim to reduce car travel, both within the town and from the community to the rest of the city. To achieve this, they have to be situated close to fast rail or bus links into the city centre and to other parts of the city.

PERSPECTIVE

Greenfield or brownfield sites?

Many environmentalists question whether eco-towns are truly sustainable. They are opposed to destroying green fields and countryside to build them and say they should be built only on brownfield sites, such as disused airfields, old collieries and other sites previously used by industry or commerce. They argue that it is more sustainable to build smaller eco-communities in many different towns and cities, where there are already transport links and other services. They point out that all new building should be sustainable.

SUSTAINABLE CITIES

When allocating housing, many eco-communities give priority to people who do not own cars. Instead they encourage all residents to walk or cycle by providing cycle routes and pleasant, safe walking routes around the community.

Working close to home

Many suburbs and commuter towns become like ghost towns during the day because most of the residents travel to work elsewhere. In the past, it was healthier and safer to build homes well away from factories that belched out smoke and poisonous gases. However, many countries today have far fewer factories so it is not always necessary to separate work and home. Eco-communities are increasingly including offices and other workplaces within their schemes. Working close to home not only cuts down on travelling but it also makes the community livelier during the day. Parents can spend more time with their children and be more flexible about the hours they work.

This bank in Heidelberg, Germany, has large solar panels on the roof that generate electricity for use inside the building.

Sustainable buildings

It is difficult to make large buildings totally carbon free, but it is possible to design sustainable buildings using a mixture of low-tech and high-tech features. For example, a building can be designed to use as much natural daylight as possible, and so save electricity. Computers can monitor the temperature and lighting in each room and adjust them so that they are kept comfortable without wasting electricity. Some buildings use innovative ways of saving energy. A nightclub in London, for example, has special crystals in the floor that produce electricity when people dance on them!

Computers that have LCD monitors use 77 per cent less energy than older monitors. They are also more comfortable to work with because they have less glare and emit less radiation.

SUSTAINABLE TECHNOLOGIES

Eco-city council offices

In 2006 Melbourne City Council opened a new ten-storey council building called Council House 2 (or CH2). It was designed to save energy and water. The building uses fresh air instead of air conditioning. It has photovoltaic cells and six wind turbines to generate electricity. It also has a micro-turbine to generate extra electricity to heat water for the building. Rainwater is collected, and waste water is recycled. These and other features mean that CH2 uses only 30 per cent of the water and 15 per cent of the energy of a conventional office building.

CHAPTER 5

Making Existing Cities Greener

The problems of climate change and decreasing supplies of resources are so immediate that we cannot wait for new buildings to gradually make cities sustainable. Cities also have to reduce the amount of energy and resources that existing buildings use.

The owners of this old house have placed photovoltaic cells over the roof to generate electricity.

To achieve this, national governments, local councils and city residents need to work together. Governments and local councils could take the lead, setting targets and giving advice. They should also give money to people who cannot afford to pay for the necessary changes themselves.

Adapting buildings

Luckily, many of the devices and techniques used in eco-buildings also work in conventional buildings. Solar water heaters and photovoltaic cells can both be added to existing roofs. The most suitable roofs are those that face towards the midday sun. On flat roofs, the panels and cells are tilted to catch the most sunshine. In some places, extra electricity made by PV cells is bought by an electricity company and fed into the national grid.

30

This building, which is being constructed from wood and natural materials, is right in the centre of Berlin, Germany. Office buildings are constantly being pulled down and redeveloped. This gives an opportunity for the new buildings to be designed to be sustainable.

Saving energy

The easiest way to save energy is to cut out waste – most people waste about a third of the energy they use. For example, traditional incandescent light bulbs burn five times as much electricity as compact fluorescent light (CFL) bulbs. A staggering 90 per cent of the electricity that traditional bulbs use is wasted as heat. CFL bulbs also last about eight times as long. Since fewer are needed, this means that less greenhouse gas is created by the production of light bulbs.

Governments can help speed up the change to CFL bulbs by banning the sale of traditional bulbs. In 2005, for example, Cuba changed all of its light bulbs to energy-saving ones. The Australian government announced in 2007 that the sale of traditional bulbs would be banned by 2010.

Insulation

Insulation that is used in new buildings can be added to older buildings. The insulation can be glued to the outside walls. However, since about the 1920s, most homes have been built with cavity walls, which means that the outer wall consists of two walls with a space between them. Cavity walls are better insulators than single-thickness walls, and filling the cavity with insulating foam makes them better still. Insulation can be added to existing lofts, and windows can be draught-proofed and double-glazed. Although insulation costs money, it also saves money by reducing heating bills.

SUSTAINABLE TECHNOLOGIES

Efficient photovoltaic cells

Photovoltaic cells are expensive to produce and buy, but scientists at the Massachusetts Institute of Technology (MIT), USA, have devised a way of reducing the size of the PV cells and using them on windows instead of roofs. The glass windowpanes are coated with a transparent dye that collects sunlight and directs it to the cells, which are in the window frame. The technique means that each cell can produce ten times more electricity than those used on roofs.

SUSTAINABLE CITIES

This outdoor farmers' market, selling fresh carrots and celery, looks as if it is in a small market town, but it is actually in Union Square in the middle of New York, USA!

Sustainable food

Shops and residents can both play their part in reducing the amount of fuel used to bring food into the city. The further away the food comes from, the more fuel is burned in transporting it. Flying in fresh food from distant countries by aircraft produces many tonnes of greenhouse gases.

City-dwellers can help by buying locally grown food. Many shops in Britain, for example, label food to show where it comes from. Some, such as Waitrose, include an aeroplane logo on food that has been flown in. Farmers' markets are increasingly popular in many countries. Instead of selling their produce to shops and supermarkets, some farmers take it to markets in local towns and cities. The farmers get a better price for their products, and the customers can buy fresh food directly from the people who grew it.

Growing your own

The best way to eat fresh, local food is to grow your own! Wherever people live, it is usually possible to grow tomatoes, herbs and other vegetables in plant pots and window boxes. People with gardens can grow more vegetables. In Britain, cities are required to put land aside for allotments – small individual plots of land for growing fruit and vegetables. Recently, allotments have become so popular that there are often long waiting lists for them.

(opposite) An allotment holder plants lettuces in the Rotonda de Cojimar allotment garden, in Havana, Cuba.

PERSPECTIVE

Enjoying the freshest food

The fresher food is, the better it tastes. This is what one allotment holder says: 'Once you've tasted "allotment snacks" such as strawberries two seconds off their stems and exploding with taste, or raw peas sweeter than sweets, you are spoilt for life. This is "no-food-miles food" grown in soil that you have dug yourself. It doesn't get better than that!'

Changing planning laws

In the past, many councils planned cities so that some areas were mainly for homes and others for industry and commerce. It makes sense to keep oil refineries, chemical factories and any site that is noisy, or produces unhealthy or dangerous substances, away from residential areas. However, most offices are safe and clean. Where feasible, planning laws could be changed so that more people can work closer to home and so save time and fuel commuting across the city.

Recycling

Most cities are beginning to tackle the problems of waste by recycling as much of it as possible. Paper, glass, tin cans and some plastic bottles can all be recycled. Food scraps and garden waste can be made into compost. The local council sets up the system for collecting the rubbish and sorting it, but people need to use the system. Some councils require people to place their rubbish into different bins for each material. Kamikatsu, a village in south-western Japan, shows what can be done. It has a zero-waste policy, which means that all of its rubbish is recycled. To achieve this, residents have to sort their rubbish into 34 different bins!

Processing recycled materials

Most materials that are recycled are processed and used again. Once metal cans reach the recycling centre, for example, they are separated into steel and aluminium. They are then melted down and rolled into thin sheets of metal, ready to be used again. It can take just 60 days for a drinks can to be made into a new can that is filled, sold and recycled again. Recycling uses some energy, but it takes much less energy to make paper, glass and metal from recycled materials than it does from raw material.

Plastic

Plastic is the most difficult material to recycle, because there are several different kinds. In theory, most types of plastic can be recycled, but this means sorting out each kind and recycling it separately. In practice, it is usually only plastic milk and drink containers that are recycled.

FACE THE FACTS

Recycling a tonne of paper saves:

- 30,000 litres of water
- about 3,500 kilowatt hours of electricity.

Recycling a tonne of steel saves:

- 1.5 tonnes of iron ore
- 40% of the water used to make new steel
- 75% of the energy used to make new steel.

(opposite) This worker in Beijing, China, is sorting out plastic rubbish that can be recycled.

CHAPTER 6

Getting Around the City

Transport is the life-blood of a city. Vehicles move people, goods and materials from place to place and in and out of the city. Cars, motor scooters, bicycles, buses and trams compete for space with lorries and vans. The result is heavy air pollution and often traffic congestion.

The way to make cities more sustainable is to reduce the amount of traffic, especially private cars. Yet many city councils are more concerned about controlling the traffic and keeping it flowing.

Roads

Newer cities, such as Los Angeles, USA, and Singapore in China, have been built to accommodate private cars. Multi-lane highways cross the city, and shopping malls have large parking areas. Many older cities have copied this policy. Roads have been widened and flyovers built to speed traffic in and out of the city. Ring roads around and within the city help traffic to avoid the city centre. However, fast roads built to relieve congestion often attract extra vehicles and

Although Seoul in South Korea has many multi-lane highways to ease the flow of traffic, there is still congestion.

quickly become congested, too. Fast roads also create pollution and noise, and because they are difficult and unpleasant to cross, they divide communities.

Speed controls

One way to keep traffic moving is to control the speed at which it flows. Speed cameras monitor the traffic and help to identify places where congestion is building up. In quiet, residential streets, traffic is slowed down by building humps in the road or making the road narrower in places. This is called 'traffic calming' and it reduces accidents.

Discouraging cars

The richer the city, the more cars it has. City streets in poorer countries, such as India and Indonesia, are busy but less congested, because fewer people own private cars. They travel by motor scooter or bicycle instead. Rather than trying to rebuild cities to accommodate cars, many older cities are now trying to discourage people from using their cars except when essential.

SUSTAINABLE TECHNOLOGIES

Car sharing

London is one city where car-sharing schemes are growing fast. Instead of owning their own car, people who join the scheme have access to a pool of cars, which they book and pay for by the hour. The scheme works best for people who can switch to using public transport and only need a car occasionally.

Bicycles are cheap, carbon-free to ride, and very versatile. This trader on the island of Java in Indonesia is transporting several cages of birds on his bicycle.

SUSTAINABLE CITIES

Parking restrictions

The easiest way to dissuade people from using their cars in a city is to make parking difficult and more expensive. Parking may be limited to car parks and to parking spaces on the street that have to be paid for. Instead of putting money into a parking meter, the latest schemes allow drivers to pay for parking by credit card using their mobile phones. In some places, residents have to buy a special permit to park in the street outside their home. This prevents non-residents from parking there.

Car-free zones

Some cities have gone even further – they have banned cars from the city centre. City centres are usually the oldest part of a city. The streets are often narrow

Shoppers and tourists stroll along pedestrianized streets in the centre of Barcelona, Spain.

and easily become clogged with traffic. Some cities have reclaimed parts of their city centres for pedestrians by making whole streets and areas car-free, so allowing people to wander safely and freely.

Congestion charging

Many cities are too large to keep cars out of the entire city centre. London was the first city to try a new plan – every car that drives into the centre has to pay a daily congestion charge. Instead of driving in by car, people are encouraged to use public transport and to cycle or walk.

Cycle tracks

Cycling is healthy and produces no greenhouse gases or pollution. Cycling in a city can be dangerous, however, particularly along fast roads. City councils can encourage people to cycle by planning cycle routes and making cycle tracks. Cycle routes are signposted routes that avoid the busiest roads. Cycle tracks are designed to separate bicycles from the rest of the traffic. In some cities, the track is a section of the road marked off by white lines. Even better are the cycle tracks in cities such as Copenhagen, which are separate from both roads and pavements.

FACE THE FACTS

Between August 2005 and July 2006, Stockholm, the capital of Sweden, brought in congestion charging for a trial period. At the same time, public transport was improved. It was found that during the trial:

- Rush-hour traffic was reduced by 20–25%
- Time spent queuing in traffic jams was reduced by 30–50%
- Air pollution was reduced by 14%.

Bicycle taxis, such as this one in Tokyo in Japan, are common in many countries in Asia. They are now being used in cities in Europe and North America too.

SUSTAINABLE CITIES

Improving public transport

The key to persuading people to leave their cars at home is a fast, reliable and cheap public transport system. Public transport – buses, trams and trains – declined as the number of cars in cities increased. If cities are to become more sustainable, governments and city councils need to spend money to improve these services.

Buses

Buses have the huge advantage that they run on existing streets and roads. The challenge is to help them avoid traffic jams and run regularly and reliably. One way to do this is to create special bus lanes. A bus lane is a section of the road that is reserved for buses, and often taxis and cyclists, too. In many cities, buses are linked to a GPS navigation system, which informs passengers waiting at bus stops when the next bus is due.

FACE THE FACTS

Most US cities are dominated by cars, but Portland in Oregon has one of the best public transport systems in the world. One Portland family accepted a challenge to give up their SUV for a month and travel only by public transport. They were so surprised at how easy it was to get around the city using the light railway, buses, streetcars, cycle lanes and free city centre transport that they decided to sell their SUV!

London is famous for its red double-decker buses – bus routes criss-cross the city. Bus lanes and a pre-pay fare system have greatly helped to speed up travelling by bus.

Trams

Trams, powered by overhead electric cables, also use the streets but they run on special rails. In the past, many cities had cheap tram services, but the rails were pulled up because they got in the way of cars. In recent years, many cities have set up new tram services. They cause less air pollution than buses, but they are only truly sustainable if the electricity they use is generated without producing greenhouse gases.

Trains

Trains are the fastest form of public transport. Many cities have underground as well as overground trains. Some cities, for example in Germany, have railway systems that run above the street on elevated tracks. Most railway lines were built to run from the edge of the city into the centre. Now cities need to add new lines so that people can move across the city as well.

Modern trams speed past road traffic in Barcelona, Spain. Planners in the city realized that they could set up a tram system more cheaply and quickly than an underground rail system.

CHAPTER 7

Better for Everyone

Making cities more sustainable is good for everyone. Sustainable cities benefit the world by consuming fewer resources and producing fewer greenhouse gases. They benefit residents because they are healthier and less stressful places to live.

These cities put people in touch with the wider environment by making them more aware of the materials and energy they use. Plants, trees and green spaces play an essential part by providing a direct link with the natural world.

Importance of trees
Many city streets are lined with trees and shrubs. During daylight hours, their green leaves take in carbon dioxide from the air and release oxygen, making the air cleaner and healthier to breathe. In summer they shade the pavements and the buildings. They soften the hard edges and surfaces of streets and buildings, bringing a reminder of the natural world. Street trees can be cut back from time to time so that they do not take up too much space and to prevent their roots from damaging buildings.

SUSTAINABLE TECHNOLOGIES

A pleasant working environment

The ING Bank building in Amsterdam was designed to save energy and provide the best possible working environment for its employees. It includes art, natural materials and water features. The building is surrounded by gardens with running water, and every worker sits within seven metres of a window. Mirrors in the ceilings reflect the daylight to make the rooms even brighter.

Parks and gardens

Parks are invaluable to city-dwellers. They are quiet and peaceful places away from the bustle and noise of the streets, where people can walk or simply sit and think. They provide space for jogging, playing football and many other healthy activities. Parks have enough space to allow trees to grow to their full height, providing food for birds, squirrels and many kinds of insects. In summer, they create shade for people.

Lakes and waterways

Many parks and public gardens include lakes or large ponds. They attract ducks and other waterfowl. Many cities are rediscovering old waterways – streams, rivers and canals – which were once used to transport goods. Opening up the paths alongside waterways creates interesting and unusual nature walks – a sliver of countryside through the middle of a city.

Singapore has a treetop walk through natural rainforest on high ground in the middle of the city. The 10-km walk gives views of the city below and of birds, monkeys and other wildlife in the trees.

GLOSSARY

argon A colourless gas that does not react with other substances.

commuter town A town where most of the residents travel to nearby cities to work.

compact fluorescent light (CFL) bulb An energy-saving light bulb that produces light when electricity is passed through a gas, making it glow.

compost The rotten remains of plants and living things that can be used as a fertilizer.

congestion Overcrowding on the roads, which causes traffic jams.

consumer goods Goods, such as televisions, washing machines and clothes, that make life more comfortable.

developing countries Poorer countries, where a smaller percentage of people work in factories and offices than in richer countries.

drought A prolonged period with little or no rain.

eco-home A home that produces few or no greenhouse gases and less damage to the environment than other homes.

ecological footprint A measure of the area of land needed to provide each person with everything he or she consumes and to dispose of the waste produced.

fertilizer Substances added to the soil to feed plants and make them grow better.

filtered Passed through charcoal, sand or other substances in order to remove impurities.

gigawatt A measure of electricity equal to a million watts.

GPS navigation system A way of tracking vehicles using a global positioning satellite. A receiver on the vehicle is linked to a control room via the satellite.

greenhouse gases Gases in the atmosphere that trap the sun's heat.

grey water Water that is not clean enough to drink but is clean enough for other purposes, such as watering the garden.

hurricane A tropical storm that begins over the ocean and develops spiralling winds of more than 118 km per hour and heavy rain.

hydrogen fuel cell A device that generates electricity by combining hydrogen with oxygen.

incinerator A furnace that reduces rubbish and other things to ash.

Industrial Revolution A period in history between about 1750 and 1850 when industry developed rapidly and goods began to be made in large quantities in factories.

insulate To prevent the movement of heat from one place to another.

landfill System of disposing of rubbish by burying it in the earth.

malaria A disease spread by infected mosquitoes.

methane A greenhouse gas that traps 20 times as much heat as carbon dioxide, weight for weight. It is an efficient fuel and is the main ingredient of natural gas.

pesticide A chemical used to kill pests on crops and livestock.

photochemical smog Smog produced by the action of sunlight on pollution.

photovoltaic (PV) cell A device that changes sunlight into electricity.

raw material A substance in its natural state, such as wood, mineral ores and oil, that is used to make goods.

recycling Processing unwanted materials so that they can be used again.

renewable Able to be renewed. Wind and sunlight, for example, are renewable sources of energy because they will not run out.

resource A supply of something, such as crops, coal and water, that can be used to satisfy a need.

FURTHER INFORMATION

shanty town Unofficial settlement that people build near or in a city.

slum An area of a city that is very poor and where the houses are in a bad condition.

solar water heater A device that uses the heat of the sun to heat water.

suburb An area of a city that is outside the city centre.

sustainable Able to keep going. A sustainable city does not use resources faster than they can be replaced or renewed.

sustainable energy Energy that comes from sustainable or renewable sources, such as wind and the power of the sun.

SUV (Sports Utility Vehicle) A large, powerful car that can be driven off-road.

thatch Roofing material made from straw, reeds or other plants.

unsustainable Using resources faster than they can be replaced or renewed.

ventilation Replacement of used air with fresh air.

wholesaler A person who buys goods in large quantities and sells them on in small quantities.

wind turbine A device for generating electricity using the power of the wind.

Website disclaimer
Note to parents and teachers: Every effort has been made by the publishers to ensure that these websites are suitable for children, that they are of the highest educational value, and that they contain no inappropriate or offensive material. However, because of the nature of the Internet, it is impossible to guarantee that the contents of these sites will not be altered. We strongly advise that Internet access is supervised by a responsible adult.

BOOKS

Building a Green Community, Ellen Rodger, Crabtree Publishing, 2008

Earth in Danger: Climate Change, Helen Orme, Bearport Publishing, 2008

Eco-Action: Buildings of the Future, Angela Royston, Heinemann Library, 2008

Eyewitness: Climate Change, John Woodward, Dorling Kindersley, 2008

Sustainable World: Cities, Roy Bowden, KidHaven Press, 2004

WEBSITES

http://geography.about.com/library/weekly/aa011201g.htm
Gives statistics on the largest cities over the last 5,000 years.

http://science.nasa.gov/headlines/y2002/solarcells.htm
NASA website: how photovoltaic cells work.

http://www.energysavingtrust.org.uk
Explore this website to find out how homes can be improved to save energy and how they can generate their own electricity.

http://www.epa.gov/climatechange/
United States Environmental Protection Agency website on climate change.

http://www.greenhomebuilding.com/earthship.htm
All about the different materials that are used to build Earthships.

http://www.greenpeace.org.uk/efficiencity/about
Efficiencity is a virtual sustainable town created on the Greenpeace website. Click for an interactive visit to the town to see how it works.

http://www.prb.org/Articles/2007/623Urbanization.aspx
Looks at increasing urbanization of the world's population and the effect of cities on the environment.

http://www.wasteonline.org.uk/index.aspx
Gives information and statistics about savings made by recycling different materials.

INDEX

adobe buildings 19, **19**
allotments 32, **33**
architects 7, 17, 18, 19

bicycle taxis **39**
Britain 26, 32
brownfield sites 27
buses 40, **40**

car-free zones 38–9
car sharing 37
cars 11, 27, 36, 37, 38, 39, 40
China 9, **25**, 27, **34**
combined heat and power stations 27
compact fluorescent light bulbs 31
compost 24, 25
compost toilet 24
computers 29, **29**
congestion 36, **36**, 37
congestion charge 39
councils 29, **29**, 35, 36, 39, 40
Cuba 31, **33**
cycle tracks 39
cycling 28, 37, **37**, 39

draught-proofing 23, 31

earthshelter 23, **23**
Earthships 18, **18**, 19
eco-communities 26, **26**, 27, **27**, 28
eco-homes 18, **18**, 19–20, 22, 23, **23**, 24, 25
ecological footprint 13
eco-towns 26, 27
electricity 11, 12, 20, 27, 29, 30, 31

farmers' markets 32, **32**
farming 8
flooding 17
food 17, 25, 32, **33**
fossil fuels 16, 17
Freiburg, Germany 26

Gandhi, Mahatma 13
gardens 24, 25, **25**, 32, 43
global warming 16, 17
governments 30, 31, 40
greenhouse effect **16**
greenhouse gases 16, **16**, 31, 32

Hangzhou, China 9
Harrall, Jerry 23
heat pumps 20
history of cities 8, **8**, 9, **9**, 10–11
homes 11, **11**, 12 (see also eco-homes)

incinerators 14
Industrial Revolution 10
insulation 19, 22, **22**, 23, 31

lakes 43
landfill sites 14
London 13, 37

Melbourne, Australia 29, **29**
Mohenjo-Daro **8**
mud buildings 19, **19**

New Orleans 17
New York 7, 13, **32**

oil 11, 17, 22
Olympic Village, Sydney, Australia 26, **26**

parking restrictions 38
parks 43, **43**
photovoltaic cells 20, **21**, 29, 30, **30**, 31
planning, city 35
plastic **34**, 35
pollution 15, **15**, 37, 39
Polo, Marco 9
population, urban 7, 8, 9, 10, **10**
public transport 40–41, **40–41**

recycling 18, 24, 29, **34**, 35
Reynolds, Michael 18, 19
roads 36, **36**, 37
rubbish 14, **14**, **34**, 35

sewage 15, 24, 25
sewerage systems 11, 15, 24
shanty towns 11, **11**, 15
skyscrapers **7**, 11
solar heating 20, **21**, **26**, 30, **30**
speed controls 37
Stockholm, Sweden **27**, 39

toilets 24
Tokyo-Yokohama, Japan 7, **12**, **13**, **15**, 39
trade 8, 9
traffic 36, 37, 39
trains 41
trams 41, **41**
transport 11, 17, 27, 36–7, **36–7**, 38–41, **39–41**
trees 19, 20, 42, 43

ventilation, natural 23

waste 14, **14**, 15, 24, 27, 31
 materials 18, **18**, **34**, 35
water 12, 42
 grey 24
 saving 24, 29
 shortages 17, 24
waterways 43
wildlife 43
wind catchers 23
wind turbines 20, 29
windows
 double-glazed 22, 31
 triple-glazed 22, **22**,
wood 19, 20
work 6, 17, 28, 35, 42

zero-waste policy 35

Page numbers in **BOLD** refer to illustrations and charts.